Not-Yet Elegies

by

Erin Covey-Smith

Finishing Line Press
Georgetown, Kentucky

Not-Yet Elegies

Publisher: Leah Huete de Maines

Editor: Christen Kincaid

Cover Art: Erin Covey-Smith

Author Photo: Wes Covey

Cover Design: Elizabeth Maines McCleavy

Order online: www.finishinglinepress.com
also available on amazon.com

Author inquiries and mail orders:
Finishing Line Press
P. O. Box 1626
Georgetown, Kentucky 40324
U. S. A.

*Poetry is always a dying language
and never a dead language.*

—Robert Smithson

The archaeologists found the palimpsests first,
releasing them from the earth.
Their ancient seeds caught in the wind and spread,
and sprouted.
Sprouted centuries and buildings and cities and centuries again.

The palimpsests stopped being legible (as ancient scrolls are wont to do),
effaced by time and blindness.
Instead, they whispered, whispered quietly but insistently,
persistently.

The archaeologists, heedless, dug on, seeking answers at the center of the earth,
as the palimpsest-seeds spread across the surface.
They grew roots, grew up, and looked forward (as living things are wont to do),
bearing us along on their whispers.

No longer legible,
are they audible?

Culture resides mainly in people's heads and in the examples people set, and is subject therefore to natural mortality.

—Jane Jacobs, *Dark Age Ahead*

The Unnatural Mortality of Culture:

It tripped off a cliff. (*It* is a creature concocted of predecessors.)
Running, eyes closed,
feeling the wind in its face.
Sensing, through force of propulsion (and with satisfaction),
an increasing distance from its origin.
Its restless (relentless) progress.

    (Progress dropped a stone in its pocket every stride,
    tried to slow the pace.
    Instead it tripped,
    the weight of history in its pockets.)

About three million years after distant glaciers pushed some courageous, hungry specimens of Pan prior out of forests no longer big enough to sustain us—and some of them proved imaginative enough to survive—the world warmed again.

—Alan Weisman, *The World Without Us*

I.

If imagination has allowed for survival,
and if Tolkein says despair is only for those who are *certain* of the future. . .

then.

(what?)

then there is a *Then?*
Then now is a *Not-Yet.*

(Only) imagine the possibilities.

(Remember *when?*)

II.

Some cell remembers.
Some primeval speck of inherent biology
contains a memory of imagining beyond the forest edge.

III.

We float on a sheath over despair,
says Oliver Wendell Holmes, Jr.,
and the only thing keeping us afloat is
"the sure issue and worth of effort."

A sheath that accelerates in the current,
the edge (the *Yet*) a quickening horizon.
And the waters gargle   (garble)

Try. Try to imagine.

They decided to straighten time of its round-abouts and kinks,
its cyclical way of being (its earth-bound way of being, where lie
the roots). They decided to make time make sense.

When they decided to straighten time (to clear it of obstructions in its path—its past),
they accelerated it like an arrow (like a runner).

When they decided to straighten time, they forgot about The End
(and the end makes least sense of all).

As if you could kill time without injuring eternity. . .

—Henry David Thoreau, *Walden*

Did you note that hobble in eternity?

Across the street, through a screen of traffic,
                              (what Blake would call a dirty door)
a raw, tremoring glimpse.

Or in the news last night, each story bespeaking mortality.

Did you kill time? Did I?

> *(If the doors of perception were cleansed,*
> *everything would appear to man as it is:*
> *infinite.)*

Because I just felt eternity lurch.

In the city,
the number of times streetlights, sign-lights, plane-lights,
moonlight, starlight, celestial lights
are conflated, mistaken,
one for the other.

When we are at an age to imagine, we cannot say how or why we imagine. Then, when we could say how we imagine, we cease to imagine. We should therefore dematurize ourselves.

—Gaston Bachelard, *Poetics of Space*

How, Gaston Bachelard,
how?

How to untie, untangle, unknot history;
how to regress to some immature, originary dreamer,
sitting on a stump, in the childhood of the world,
imagining the possibilities.

Or is it so necessary?
Did the dreamer seep through the knots and tangles, (the roots)
embed himself somewhere around here,
in a world that becomes, and becomes, and becomes?

The world has reached a ripe old age, it is true. It can not(?) be undone.

Can we?

.

Two women in the doctor's office casually, a bit flippantly, discuss The End Of Time. They give a little laugh, a little sigh, and move on to topics of more immediate interest.

(But they hear it, don't they? And laugh where there are no words.)

The debris of shipwrecked histories still today raise up the ruins of an unknown, strange city. They burst forth within the Modernist, massive, homogeneous city like slips of the tongue from unknown, perhaps unconscious language.

—de Certeau and Giard, *The Practice of Everyday Life: Living and Cooking*

Wendell Holmes' sheath (a flimsy construct, really) has been shipwrecked before. Yet it floats on, over roiling waters. (Which occasionally, from their depths, issue a shard, a fragment, a memory.)

(dirty doors)

I don't know.
I see sage old dreams all around.
They crouch in the sidewalk slush and the shadiest alleyways.

(They whisper.)

How to imagine something else when there is no way to conceive of what *is?*
How to imagine the pleisto-mio-paleo-oligo-cene eras,
so many stones in the pocket?

The rise and fall of empires?

(The 7.8 billion of us.)

It is replete, this world crammed with space and time.   (Doesn't it seem?)
Must one, then, imagine Nothing?
Dream the invisible—
the only substance to fill in the gaps because it is *Not.*

And isn't it the most dazzling *Not* you've ever seen?
(You do see it, don't you?)

From one part to the other, the city seems to continue, in perspective, multiplying its repertory of images: but instead it has no thickness, it consists only of a face and an obverse, like a sheet of paper, with a figure on either side, which can neither be separated nor look at each other.

—Italo Calvino, *Invisible Cities*

You describe, Marco Polo, the Janus-faced city
of alabaster and rust.

Except (Marco Polo) perhaps it is not so simply one or the other.
Perhaps they are thick with each other,
thick in the midst of the all-at-once.
Rusting sheet metal and glass towers
layer upon layer, confronting each other each day.

In the Janus-faced city,
the rust appears comfortable, (maybe a bit resigned)
knowing it is where it will be.
The tower shivers in the wind,
knowing where it is to go.

Look! exclaims the child on the city bus, *the graveyard, it's so beautiful!*
(in the snow, each grave wearing a cap)

Uninhibited.

Like hearing astronomers explain the entire universe, its lessons get lost because its subject, when it was alive, literally exceeded our horizons. The postmortem of the American passenger pigeon is so fertile with portents that just a brief glance warns—screams, in fact—that anything we consider limitless probably isn't.

—Alan Weisman, *The World Without Us*

I.

There are 7.8 billion of us.
I means nothing.   (*I* is speck of biology.)

What to care about in lieu of nothing, in lieu of *me?*
What to listen to when whispers are audible as screams,
screams audible as whispers?

(What? All of it.)

II.

Don't you see it, hear it (know it, breathe it, live it), this imminent peril?
The resounding *yes* of 7.8 billion people, thousands of languages:
cacophony.

(Or, a laugh.)

Kids are hopeless. Until their parents, peers, and the education system brainwash them to start planning and hoping for their future and living inside their heads, they live in the present—without hope. By listening to them we can relearn what it means to live without the need to hope, just to accept and be.

—Dave Pollard, *"10 Things to do When You're Feeling Hopeless"*

Utopia, they say, is a hopeless world, replete with dreams.
(Utopia is a paradox only children understand.)

To reach Utopia, they say, you simply re-learn. You simply de-maturize.

(Simply, you turn back time.)

A clear-skied moon tonight
(through streaked glass, through the mesh of a window screen).

It was as if plastic exploded upon the world from a tiny seed after World War II and, like the Big Bang, was still expanding.

—Alan Weisman, *The World Without Us*

(seeds on the wind)

Forces of nature,
forced nature.
Naturally, forced into being.

And being, and being. . . and being.

(and imploding.)

In this model, culture spreads like the surface of a body of water, spreading towards available spaces or trickling downwards towards new spaces through fissures and gaps, eroding what is in its way.

—"Rhizome," *Wikipedia*

A tenacious, invisible root took hold, beneath it all,
  (a potato, a ginger-root)
in some timeless time.
  (down, where the archaeologists dig)

Tenacious but benign, benevolent, nourishing,
whispering encouragement.

Sprouting

something else, insidious, corrosive, slick across the surface,
liquid, seeking fissures.

  (fissures blocked
   with discarded plastic bags.)

                    Was Janus responsible for planting such growths? Janus,
                    knowing duality, knowing impossible, undetterable
                    coexistence so well.

Then again, this morning, the sticking door of a municipal building in the sonorous, deceptive pitch of a bird call.

Were you thinking that those were the words, those
*   upright lines? those curves, angles, dots?*
No, those are not the words, the substantial words are in
*   the ground and sea,*
They are in the air, they are in you.
I speak not, yet if you hear me not of what avail am I to
*   you?*

—Walt Whitman, *"A Song of the Rolling Earth"*

They've been there all along.
All else has rolled under, but they continue to surface
  (surface in the strangest places, surface in the streetlights in lieu of stars).

Surface and try, try to say Something,
using no language so all tongues may understand.
  (using an *unknown, perhaps unconscious language*)

It is a huge, a *substantial,* silence.
We have no more room for vast silence.
We understand too much to understand these words.

                  (And thus must un-understand?)

A child is hopeless.
A potato is a rhizome.
Simplicity does not look forward, and somehow this is wise.

To name an object is to destroy three quarters of the enjoyment of a poem, which is given to be guessed little by little: to suggest, that is the dream.

—Stéphane Mallarmé, *Enquête sur l'évolution littéraire*

We seem to have a poem on our hands.
  (We seem to have created a poem with our hands, all of them together,
  our hands full of history.)

We seem to have, in Umberto Eco's words,
  worked out an authentic metaphysics of poetic creation,
simply by being born, by proliferating so prolifically.
  (So profoundly.)

By enduring.

Certainly, it can only be guessed at.
Certainly, we are full of suggestions (and few answers.)
Occasionally, there is a glimpse—
a root pokes through.

(*Enjoyable?* This ineffability? Perhaps it is an elegy we have on our hands,
we have made with our hands.
Magical? At least we imagined it so—when the root poked through.
The Utopoem.)

At WIPP, where much of [decommissioned nuclear defense facility] Rocky Flats ended up, the U.S. Department of Energy is legally required to dissuade anyone from coming too close for the next 10,000 years.

—Alan Weisman, *The World Without Us*

They are sealing nuclear waste underground (with the ginger-root),
and devising ways of communicating its danger to future generations
whose language will have morphed.

What would Walt Whitman say?

Another language, all mixed up in the earth.
Another mystery for future archaeologists.

Is this our whispered response, our response to the whisper?

(This is a heavy stone for a pocket to hold.)

On the spurious map of the future presented herein, on the far side of the pinpoint of now, I have to inscribe, as did the medieval cartographers over all the terrifying areas outside their ken: HERE LIVE LIONS.

—Bernard Wolfe, *Limbo '90*

How to live on a pinpoint?

        (Precariously, with a great deal of balance and concentration.)

A pinpoint crowded with archaeologists and medieval cartographers.

        (I am an archaeologist, I am a cartographer. So, I venture to guess, are you.)
        Digging into yesterday's tomorrows (past *Yets*),
        heedlessly seeking unheeded answers,
        all the while propelled, impelled forward.

All the while teetering (terrified) on the edge, on the pinpoint,
of the *Not-Yet*.
But not falling,

        yet.

        (Yet, children frolic on this pinpoint,
        uninhibited.)

Paul Kennedy: "...I would like to ask each of these people who are economic experts, what they understand to be the time line. How long do we have?"

Peter Victor:"... I think it's clear to say we have reached the point when we can no longer act quickly. Acting quickly is something we could have done 25, 30, 40 years ago. We've missed the chance to act quickly... So if you ask me time line, in respect to many issues, we have left it too late."

—CBC Radio, *Ideas With Paul Kennedy*

The Powers That Be Impel Bad Grammar

I needn't take the blame
         (for I am a speck of biology).
I am not *we*.

When I try to point at *we, we* dissipates,
dissolves.
         (7.8 billion specks of nothing.)

I could resolve the issue thus:
The experts claim that for any hope of salvation, something
needed to be done yesterday.

But then we have a passive voice. We have no agent.
         (*We* has no agency).

Who was to do that Something?

Who is in charge here?
         (Who is *we*?)

Who is the agent to activate yesterday?

                              (Who can turn back time?)

"Humans are going extinct eventually. Everything has, so far. It's like death: there's no reason to think we're any different. But life will continue. It may be microbial life at first. Or centipedes running around. Then life will get better and go on, whether we're here or not. I figure it's interesting to be here now," he says. *"I'm not going to get all upset about it."*
[Doug Erwin, paleobiologist]

—Alan Weisman, *The World Without Us*

Dear archaeologists, dear cartographers:

This human mark, what is this?
Perhaps we should be paleobiologists instead, paleobiologists
who look not only beyond the forest edge but beyond 7.8 billion.

The view from the strata of history is opaque with roots and mysteries.
The view from the pinpoint of now, vertiginous and rife with lions.
The view from outside human time is not so grim.

(The view from all sides is interesting, nonetheless.
All of it, compelling, impelling.)

The newscasters report statistics
cold and hard like apartment blocks.
And then they move on to the weather.

(The statistics haul the *Yet*, ungainly, up onto this pinpoint, this *Not-*, and cause
a wobble.
A wobble in eternity.)

Erin Covey-Smith holds an MFA in printmaking and book arts from Concordia University in Montreal. She now writes and works as a graphic designer from her home in Maine. Her poetry may be found in *A Dangerous New World: Maine Artists on Climate Change* (2019) and in the *Goose River Anthology* (2020), among other publications; this is her debut book of poetry.

www.ingramcontent.com/pod-product-compliance
Lightning Source LLC
Chambersburg PA
CBHW021204090426
42740CB00008B/1231